BURNING THE
ASPERN PAPERS

For Richard,
    Thanks for all
the help you've given
me — and the pleasure of your poems.
With much affection
    and admiration,

    John
    10/8/2003

The Miami University Press Poetry Series
General Editor: James Reiss

The Bridge of Sighs, Steve Orlen
People Live, They Have Lives, Hugh Seidman
This Perfect Life, Kate Knapp Johnson
The Dirt, Nance Van Winckel
Moon Go Away, I Don't Love You No More, Jim Simmerman
Selected Poems: 1965-1995, Hugh Seidman
Neither World, Ralph Angel
Now, Judith Baumel
Long Distance, Aleda Shirley
What Wind Will Do, Debra Bruce
Kisses, Steve Orlen
Brilliant Windows, Larry Kramer
After a Spell, Nance Van Winckel
Kingdom Come, Jim Simmerman
Dark Summer, Molly Bendall
The Disappearing Town, John Drury
Wind Somewhere, and Shade, Kate Knapp Johnson
The Printer's Error, Aaron Fogel
Gender Studies, Jeffrey Skinner
Ariadne's Island, Molly Bendall
Burning the Aspern Papers, John Drury

BURNING THE
ASPERN PAPERS

John Drury

John Drury

Miami University Press
Oxford, Ohio

Library of Congress Cataloging-in-Publication Data

Drury, John Philip, 1950-
    Burning the Aspern papers / John Drury
        p. cm.
    ISBN 1-881163-41-5 (alk. paper) -- ISBN 1-881163-42-3 (alk. paper)
    1. Venice (Italy) - Poetry
        I. Title.
PS3554.R83 B87 2003
811'.54--dc21   2002070924

The paper in this book meets the guidelines
for permanence and durability of the Committee
on Production Guidelines for Book Longevity
of the Council on Library Resources. ∞

Printed in the U.S.A.

9 8 7 6 5 4 3 2 1

ACKNOWLEDGMENTS

Poems in this collection have appeared in the following periodicals:

The American Poetry Review: "Ghazal of Birthdays" and "Ghazal of the Messengers"
The Beloit Poetry Journal: "How It Matters"
Boulevard: "Ghazal of Landmarks"
The Chattahoochee Review: "House on the Chesapeake"
The Cortland Review: "First Trip to Venice"
Epoch: "Bamboo"
High Plains Literary Review: "Apartment Building Corridors" and "On Location"
The Journal: "Hot Spell"
Kansas Quarterly/Arkansas Review: "Blues in the Nation's Capital"
The Literary Review: "The Cemetery Island"
The New Republic: "Stadium"
The Paris Review: "Beard," "Burning the Aspern Papers," and "Ghazal for Baron Corvo"
Poetry Northwest: "The Coming On"
Shenandoah: "Li Po in Chinatown"
The Southern Review: "Aesop Revisited," "Dirty Poem," and "Ghazal of Eros"
Tar River Poetry: "Suicide Bridge"
Verse: "Ghazal of Sleeping In"
Western Humanities Review: "Pursuing the Delta Blues" and "Semester Abroad"

"Ghazal for Laurie," "Ghazal of an Island," "Ghazal of Baseball," "Ghazal of Night Sounds," "Ghazal of the Tides," and "Ghazal of the Weekend" first appeared in *Ravishing DisUnities: Real Ghazals in English,* edited by Agha Shahid Ali (Wesleyan University Press, 2000).

"Burning the Aspern Papers" received the Bernard F. Conners Prize for Poetry from *The Paris Review.*

I want to thank Andrew Hudgins, Richard Howard, and Laurie Henry for their editorial suggestions and encouragement. Murray Bodo, Pat Mora, and Norma Jenckes offered helpful advice and hospitality. I am grateful to the Charles Phelps Taft Memorial Fund of the University of Cincinnati for grants that supported the writing of this book.

TABLE OF CONTENTS

I

II

III

IV

For my mother

I

PURSUING THE DELTA BLUES

Testing one, two, three, the engineer
played back in a hotel studio, the floor
mazed with microphones, metal tape reels, booms and wire,
baffles to mute sound, a monster tape recorder.
I'll scope out all the juke joints, every bar
and roadhouse, midnight depots, and there, somewhere,
tobacco juice on his overalls, eyes a blur,
I'll have him strum, wail, coo, bark, roar.

Forget it, the devil snapped, how do you think
his thumb and palm plunk chords on low strings
as fingers pick a whine on the steel's edge? The gift's
not his. I wanted him null and void, soul stripped
of faith, hailing me at the crossroads, no, the rim
of a quarry, no, the trestle when a train whistle
scatters the bats. The truest blues won't stick
to tape. Losing means getting it:

Let me stay out till the headlights disappear.
Let me stay out till the heavens disappear.
　　I want to hear what no men living hear.
Down to the flooded river, I'll drive my car.
Down to the river, I'll drive my stolen car.
　　I'll stand on the hood and dive where drowned men are.
When I come up, I might be anywhere.
If I come up again, most anywhere,
　　I bet there won't be much I'm fit to wear.
　　　　Just air. Just air. Just air.

BLUES IN THE NATION'S CAPITAL

When the blind woman played her slide guitar
    and grumbled, a low moan with words,
I thought it was sad how she begged there, poor
    lady, bandanna on her head,
a mongrel in a broken harness curled
    by the crate she sat on, her checked
skirt nearly covering the wood. She slurred and growled
    and slid a steel bar up the neck.

I tried to place some change in her coin bin
    without making noise, but she stared
and nodded, her fingers stinging the high strings.
    I punched in late at Men's Wear
and stacked packets of shirts in even piles
    of lemon, lavender. The boss
and I took inventory, marked down tags for sales,
    descended to the cave-like warehouse.

    Bored at work, I understood
        nothing she played was sad—
she wasn't begging, she was bragging
with hot coals in her mouth, bending the wires
to her own dark shape, all grace notes and snarls.
    I wondered how she lived, shrugging
I'd never know. But I saw an Army cot,
    a braided rug
    where the dog slept, a hot plate,
and an El Producto box with coiled guitar strings
    she needled through tuning pegs,
turning until she heard the true pitch ring.

STADIUM

The women behind us are rating
    the players' cute butts,
finagling the opera glasses
from our friend, the birdwatcher,
    who's trying to determine
    the species of martin
reeling and swooping past the mezzanine.

You can't swat the gnats away, a haze
    in the ball park's
smoky glow, without a scorecard.
Elsewhere on the upper deck,
    a child has dripped the hot cheese
    of nachos on the hair,
silver and slicked, of a sleepy-eyed man.

    What I remember of games
is this: not the slides or the circus catches
or the long drives tipped into the bullpen
    but the beer spilled
on box seats of safety patrols,
and the fans racing out on the field,
    and the rain delays, everyone huddled
by the lit concession stands, and a welcome breeze
shooting through the gaps of entry ramps
    with a burst of lush mist.

ON LOCATION

If I were on a movie crew
    I'd like to be the location scout,
hunting for a colonnade
    shaded with honey locust—
or a lemon grove
    with a windmill creaking
over sheep—or a hock shop
    with gingerbread cornices.
I'd phone to say, *No,*
    still looking, and try out
all the park fountains, all
    the soda fountains in pharmacies.

For a scene of quarreling, I'd find
    an avenue where vendors hawk
religious icons. For a walk
    during which the hero
uncovers a blind boy
    weeping in a leaf pile,
I'd come upon a park
    behind the Presidential palace.
For a random murder,
    I'd wander through the French
wing of a gallery—
    marble, glass dome, vast pastel nudes.

I'd orchestrate the script: the oboes
    of fluttering blinds,
        the finger cymbals of panes.
Let the director frame each scene,
    making a box

with long fingers, peering through.
It would be my territory, any way
he turned: the harbor,
the canopied terraces, the wind.

APARTMENT BUILDING CORRIDORS

Here's to dark hallways,
    the electric carpets
where I scuffed from light to dim light,
    delivering
the news next to silver milk boxes,
    where I entered each unnumbered door
and rummaged through store rooms, open cartons
    of burst Christmas bulbs and broken lamps,
and peered at the boiler with its hellfire.

Here's to the people
    I knew about behind
blue doors with metal showing through,
    where Cora cured
a neighbor's fever with a nostrum—
    turpentine mixed with her husband's pee—
where janitor and Greek philharmonic
    conductor lived next to each other,
where children boiled chemicals in beakers.

    And here's
    to the lives I barely glimpsed
as I carried crushed boxes of Christmas cards
    door to door, scraping my fingers
        on a wall of ripples
    to neutralize the shock
when I pinched the thin knockers
    on doors that never opened,
        a flutey voice
calling "No thanks"—or not speaking at all,
    simply an eye darkening the peephole.

Dirty Poem

Whoever worships cleanliness
dwells in the canton of exclusion,
where the church walls inside are white-washed
and the dogs muzzled, the streets empty
after curfew, where crucifixes
are swaddled in gauze, and only soap
rendered from volcanic ash can scrape
the oils and smears and deep grit of earth.

But down a red stairwell, through curtains of beads,
    a singer's nipples glow through lace.
        Lovers rub lotions over aching blades.
         Coupling, they also love
    the delectable mess of sex,
        the jolt of voltage, confluence
like the clear and muddy blending
        of Potomac and Shenandoah.

Mix thoroughly—the earth tones, earthiness,
    pecks of dirt you'll eat before your death,
        the earth that hugs you or the flames
         that make you wail. O body
of flesh and fluids, O soul that revels there,
        we die for the French kiss of everything.
O pure impurity: the fleck
        of dust at the heart of each snowflake.

AESOP REVISITED

We know how the body thrives on jostling,
    jogging up escalators,
answering two phones at once, interrupting
    the stockbroker with a card trick,
partying in lofts, making love in fast taxis.

The soul, we know, binges on vistas,
    finds sequoias in bonsai,
feels lucky slipping under waterfalls
    or floating on a salt lake,
humming an endless plainsong on the prairie.

    How is it, then,
    that the body finds itself
sneezing in meadows, poison ivy
inflaming its privates, while the soul
    gags on exhaust, waits for hours
      on a subway
      platform, only
    to see the garbage train clank through?
Rodent of the body, mouse of the soul, what
cousins once removed, what fitful misfits!

SEMESTER ABROAD

In my hotel room in Grenoble
    I startle awake:
someone is calling my name
    from the street below,
out a car window, honking the horn.
    But no, there's nothing
with me in mind out there,
    just a rush of tires
and maybe footsteps growing fainter.

The morning after, I move
    to my own room,
with a slanting desk, a cylindrical
    pillow that tucks
right into the fitted sheet of the bed.
    I pull it out
each night, and lie down flat.
    I hear my neighbor,
an Iraqi, playing Pete Seeger records.

How many alps
    rise before me as I walk
and find the valley's carnival
    where a man tosses
a ring at a trough of ducks? It spins
    down the neck of one, a mallard,
    and the carny
snatches it from the water kicking and dripping
    and stuffs it into a paper bag
    and shoves the volatile parcel
    into the winner's gloved hands.

Every walk explores heaven—
        believing is seeing—
and so I venture out, even
        when I should study.
And I do. I bring a book and recite
        a phrase underneath
a lamp post, learning it by heart
        in the dark stretch
between glowings. Then I read another.

        The French student body
                is striking. Tear gas
        fogs the campus, mists
                the Calder sculpture.
They refuse to be channeled into jobs
                they didn't choose,
        just because the government
                fashioned a plan.
Dark heavy wings creak in the wind.

Wind in my face
        on the steep path to the one dining hall
still open on Sunday evening.
                When I look down
I see the severed cables swinging
        into the river. The lift
                won't be fixed
until I've left, until I've huffed up the path
        and gasped at beauty, high on steepness
        above Grenoble, my city
                of the moment, the glorious calm.

HOT SPELL

Summer torched our apartment,
our fifth-floor walkup, where both of us
hunched in the bathtub,
played Scrabble on a drawing board
balancing
on the rim, our cats patrolling the edge
and sniffing the water. Who wouldn't
spell out "sex," or "arsonist,"
given cool tiles and spaces on the grid?
We steamed in our nakedness.

In the kitchen, the plywood
floor, painted a mock-turtle green,
gave when we walked—planks
to no houseboat, no sea, buckling
from the heat
that settled in our walls, brick and bulging
plaster, though night came on, and a breeze
as jaunty as a whistler
with a zip gun in *West Side Story*
ambled by from the river.

Solace was a rental truck,
a hand from our midget landlady
tugging bundles, lugging Hefty sacks of books.
We unfurled our map,
a paper flag, the interstates
highlighted in yellow, a crooked line to the west—
away from the conflagration of bulletins, news flashes,
away from the city's constant seething—and went.

THE COMING ON

Death is like this:
vessels jamming the deep-channel harbor,
ferry, schooner, tug
in tight formation
with fire-boat and paddle-wheeler,
scow and yacht,
flowing past empty slips and wharves
glittering with broken bottles—

where I walk along,
checking my watch for the embarkment time
down a long pier
but find no liner,
the sky a vacant blue, a breeze
puffing out
my sleeves, a long stretch back to shore
and the slapdash flotilla gone.

Then I notice how narrow
the pier is, a lamp post
without a bulb at the end,
a strait of waves
before the shore where fog
has thickened, though gusts
rise up and shake
thin pilings underneath.
I lie face down, clutching
a warped, weathered plank,
toward the diminished coast.
And you are there,
stretching against me,

touching my quaking back
until it settles, calmed,
and I breathe more slowly,
waiting for nightfall.

HOUSE ON THE CHESAPEAKE

1.

      Half a football field
from the bulwark erected by Army engineers
who planned a highway never built along the bay,
across from the Eastern Shore, where I was born,
      under a baroque cathedral
of oaks, in what we called "Dracula's Castle," a bungalow
with a dormer we couldn't reach, a closed-up attic,

      behind the screen porch,
green canvas shades rolled up, on linoleum where cats
skittered and slid, near the pantry with canisters
from former tenants, lumpy beds crowding bedrooms,
      sitting at a card table pocked
with cigarette burns, I practiced solitude, training to be
alone, like the last earthling after alien landings.

It was off-season, late November, leaves crumpled
      like programs after a game,
neighbors gone, back home in the suburbs,
      the bay darkening,
      wind jarring the faded shades,
a whine through the screen that sounded like a siren
      or a spacecraft's generator.

2.

If I strolled outside,
mist and the coming dark would swallow the rickety pier,
the cavernous reaches of the bay, yachts and tankers.
Indoors, a study lamp blessed my games, tables
    of numbers scratched in pencil,
dice rattling in a cup. When a cat stretched out
on my scoresheet, I drifted off, taken with other lures,

    A Study in Scarlet
my encyclopedia as I scouted and scoured
the neighborhood, turning up scraps with runny ink
delicate as watercolors. I taped the jags
    in a cellophane mosaic
and tried to puzzle out the language of adults. I studied
a handbook for detectives: con jobs, sex offenses.

With baby powder, I lifted the fingerprints
    of relatives from flatware,
hid a tape recorder in the hamper,
      pricked my thumb to coax
    a sample of blood, smearing it
on a slide but observing, through the microscope,
    the feathery planet of my eye.

3.

  Up in the heavens,
gods may dwell—the archer and the strongman—but God
is elsewhere. Boosters detached, retro-rockets fired,
and I trained myself to visit outer space,
    itching to be an astronaut,
learning velocity and arc by punting footballs
into tangled limbs of winter trees, devising checklists

    of endurance trials.
One: ride the clackety roller coaster, paint crumbling
on its trestles. Two: take a bath in ice-cold water
and have a witness sign the official form.
    Three: eat nothing for a day
and stay in a cardboard box as long as possible.
But in the night, lying on the pier in summer,

my training petered out, waves pushing underneath
    the warped planks, constellations
lost in the vast sprinkle of reactors
    like salt pinched and tossed
    over my shoulder for luck.
Blessed with good fortune, I was magnified, acolyte
    of the dazzling planetarium.

4.

I long for the house
in a county with legalized gambling, slot machines
in the grocery stores, our tract closed in on both sides
with alleyways just wide enough to run through,
    an outdoor shower, a bed
of periwinkles, a driveway crunching as our car pulled in,
hammocks slung between oaks. I long for what never was:

    trips and trysts, entries
at midnight, panties soft as petals dropping to the floor,
sessions of trying out all the hilly beds,
and winter months I'd hole up by the furnace
    or walk the pier, a thunderstorm
crackling down the bay. How can I reconstruct what crumbles
in memory—constellations through the blasted roof?

The first step is to charm it almost back, stomp hard
    on rotting steps, clench mealy leaves,
burn vines, prop ladders on an eave
        that nearly buckles.
    Then give it up, relinquish it
to the unforgiving heavens, and say amen
    in the ruins, in the vacant space.

II

GHAZAL OF THE MESSENGERS

The Prize Patrol has inflated the balloons and loaded a raft-
    sized check in a van,
but how can they find the street where I live, a dead end with
    the sign torn down?

Crows have landed on the shade trees behind my house,
    perching there, waxy
as squat black candles. When morning hits the airwaves, the
    leaves will be gone.

Wasps in the ventilator; orb-weavers strung out across the
    garage door;
baby raccoons on the porch, chattering "go to hell"; snakes
    under the trash can.

Every night, someone's practicing a magic act, pulling a table-
    cloth from under the house,
which shifts a little, crazing and cracking on the ceiling, along
    the foundation.

Every gap on the answering machine, every hum without a
    human voice
records their message, a monotonous pitch-pipe, the Word that
    was there in the beginning stripped clean.

GHAZAL OF BIRTHDAYS

The fruit flies celebrate constantly, getting drunk on nectar,
crowding the salad bar, having sex on the aluminum brink.

The light or dark is the same, as if Monet had painted studies
of the hospital, baby after baby, wet gowns and shining forceps.

Who needs a diamond ring when we have the circulatory system
and a network of nerves like a calling circle of friends?

Somebody circled a blank square on the calendar
but wrote nothing inside, maybe the surprise of nothing.

Amazement at the sun behind clouds, the harp of light bands,
the coronation ode of this moment, driftwood at sea.

GHAZAL OF LANDMARKS

Wait long enough, and what wall isn't a wailing wall?
There's a Lion Gate in every door frame, every windowsill.

Whitman worked in a newspaper office not far from City Hall.
How many buildings have intervened? Blocks for a landfill.

At midnight, a diver plunges in the flooded quarry.
But who has mapped the outcrops of rocks in the pool?

Trilobites have traded their inland sea for sandstone.
My front porch holds fossils captive: scalloped fan, spiral.

Pandas watch bamboos flowering. The grove explodes,
and canes begin their descent when the first blossoms fall.

GHAZAL OF SLEEPING IN

Some days, at noon, I sink deeper in bed. To the world
I mutter, "Go away. Leave me here, dead to the world."

I was born to it. Aunt Delia spent her best years
propped up by pillows, preferring her bedstead to the world.

Yet strangers make love on the softest mattresses, the wind
blowing in on bare skin. Single or not, they are wed to the world.

If only a master of ceremonies ambled in, uncorking
a magnum of champagne, and toasted: "To the world!"

What sunlight, though, pries its way in through thick curtains?
What dead end in the maze of depression once led to the world?

GHAZAL OF BASEBALL

We're swatting fungoes. Jimmy swings, and there goes the baseball
up up up over the fence. That's how we lose the baseball.

I shower too late. Red splotches cover my legs and hands
from poison ivy that held, in its shadows, the baseball.

Just before sundown, when a batter conks a high fly
above trees, the sky's transparent—and so's the baseball.

Every good pitcher spins mysteries, hiding the clues, the grip
of fingers. Batters hammer him when he shows the baseball.

It's boring in right field, so I swat away gnats and look
at a rising dot until it falls and my glove swallows the baseball.

"Go to hell, Babe Ruth," yelled the Japanese soldier on the beach,
tossing his grenade the way an outfielder throws the baseball.

GHAZAL OF NIGHT SOUNDS

By the time I enter the gorge, it's dark, although voices
call from somewhere. Who's calling? It's hard to know voices.

All night long, the noises continue, but so far off I can't
make out any words. All the tugs on the river tow voices.

It's too dark to pitch a tent. I lie awake on a sleeping bag,
listening for the hidden ventriloquists who throw voices.

Through the night, every noise represents a secret vote:
birdsong or mimicking signal; barks, cries, or low voices.

The dark comes in layers: a shimmery cloak of sky, plush clouds,
needles, broad-leaves, eyelids—and behind each shadow, voices.

I think of a naked woman with Bach in the choir loft,
shadowed at evening, a harmony that needs no voices.

When the wind picks up, dark angels must be rehearsing,
a plainsong of moaning vowels in soprano voices.

GHAZAL OF THE WEEKEND

You mow the back yard and I'll rake. Then wax the floor, down
on your knees, while I swab the toilet. Mark another chore down.

Is this any way to spend a weekend? Better to kick back
and watch the Dolphins go deep–complete!–a new set of four downs.

Or send the children to a neighbor for the afternoon.
Like kids, I'll drop my shorts if you pull your underdrawers down.

It's Sunday, a day of relief, but Jehovah's Witnesses
and then a tag-team of Mormons practically knock the door down.

Sometimes I'm so close to tears, it's hard to look out the window
at the back yard, to remember what the storm tore down.

Why don't the missionaries try something new? "Have you received
Rilke into your life? His elegies might help when you're down."

Clouds move in. The grass out back is agitated by a school
of quick shadows. Soon, I hope, the heavens will pour down.

GHAZAL OF EROS

Round up all the devilish, horny men who love women
and you get a herd of jerks ready to be saved through love, women.

They gather at the roadhouse to get drunk and howl along
to the jukebox, country songs sobbing about true love, women.

While pulling off her panties, my ex-wife said, "This is the part
I always hate." And that was the first time I knew love, women.

Lightning brightens the water, the stuccoed walls. A rush
of men, over hump-backed bridges, surges toward new love, women.

Really, I consider the first time as when I didn't have to pay.
Who are the toughest critics who review love? Women.

Clothed as the day he was born again, the new convert begs
forgiveness for what he still wants: a good screw, love, women.

When my ex-wife and I broke up, we sat on her couch: "At least
we have one thing in common, John. We like to love women."

GHAZAL FOR LAURIE

Here, in the café where raucous songs blare, the white wine
calms me down. When will you get here to share the white wine?

We'll take our time by the water, birds chirping behind leaves
as other voices ebb and flow: your red hair, the white wine.

If we get a little drunk and start to kiss, or make out
like teenagers, we can blame the scent you wear, the white wine.

If your blouse comes undone, we'll take a full bottle home
and you'll dab your nipples—I'll sip there the white wine.

We'll leave the windows open to stir the gauze curtains
and take off our clothes, naked as the air, the white wine.

But I could get drunk simply floating on calm water, so you'll
be enough for this buzz—as good as (I swear) the white wine.

After a while at sea, you feel the waves even on land,
like your love an ocean away. It's a prayer, the white wine.

And just as I smuggled you into my dark hotel room, once,
when we finally pass customs, we won't declare the white wine.

GHAZAL OF THE TIDES

Atlantis is a name for the future, although the tides
rise and subside at will. As the moon goes, so go the tides.

If the city, one day, is submerged, and not paved over,
it won't be like an aquarium, with towers below the tides.

You can tell by the mud banks in the lagoon, where the sun
fires its glaze: the city will surface—when out flow the tides.

The beauty of water is its pulsing. It pulls back
only to prepare a swollen punch, a flush blow, the tides.

Then it drops back again, leaving the doorways dripping, pools
shimmering on paving stones, antiphony of yes and no, the tides.

GHAZAL OF AN ISLAND

San Francesco del Deserto

St. Francis came here by mistake, driven to land by the sea
discharging the storm's orders, on a muddy strand by the sea.

When the weather cleared, it was lovely—vines and cypresses,
a garden ready for tending, for a florist's hand by the sea.

Boys and girls once rowed here, to dance their reels and hear
squeezebox and timbrel, a hot medieval dance band by the sea.

Basta! said Francis to the birds that chattered as he prayed.
And they held their peace, obeying his command by the sea.

He plunged his walking stick in the fertile earth, a recent
cutting he had trimmed. It took root, a magic wand by the sea.

Father Antonino shows me around. "Here's where he prayed"—
and a waxy statue still prays where old walls stand by the sea.

A monk in blue jeans trims hedges, gripping gas-powered clippers,
motor buzzing with gray fumes the wind has fanned by the sea.

Across the lagoon, a man in hip boots walks on the water,
bending to dig clams where mud banks expand by the sea.

GHAZAL FOR BARON CORVO

Frederick Rolfe (1860-1913)

You shocked the English colony with your *Desire and Pursuit*
of the Whole, a handbook on how to explore desire and pursuit.

You stole the title from Plato, a likely partner in scandal,
the brains behind your grand offensive for desire and pursuit.

Like Casanova, you made love to trouble, cruising
for gondoliers, the thrust of the oar, desire and pursuit.

A platonic definition of love. But what did you love more
than Venice? Where did love demand more desire and pursuit?

In the arcades, in the ballrooms, in the canopied boats
on calm, starry nights, who could ignore desire and pursuit?

Baron, you're no aristocrat. Another name marks your island tomb.
And what's inside that locked drawer? Desire and pursuit.

III

Burning the Aspern Papers

(after Henry James)

In a Venetian palace beside a small canal, Miss Tina Bordereau sits before a fire. She holds a packet of letters written to her Aunt Juliana by an American poet named Jeffrey Aspern, who died many years ago. Until recently, a literary editor was living in the palace as a lodger, under false pretences, waiting for an opportunity to take possession of the letters. After the death of her aunt, Miss Tina suggested that she might indeed give him the "precious papers" on one condition—that he marry her. Before bolting from the palace, he stammered, "Ah Miss Tina—ah Miss Tina . . . it wouldn't do, it wouldn't do."

Tonight I spent a good while in the garden,
thinking about— well, sitting amongst the flowers
I love to see, and, when it grew too dark,
breathing in all the scents that blew, so cool
in the slight breeze, I pulled my favorite scarf
tighter around my throat. I wanted to stay
as long as I could possibly enjoy it.
I had too much to think of, as you know,
and yet could not resolve what appeared settled.
I have, now, what remains around me here
and what I have recovered from her mattress,
the papers and effects that you desired—
but not too dearly. Still, I have earned much,
my keep alone, this garden and this house,
in gold she counted, one coin, drop, one coin,
drop in the glossy box. And the key's mine.
I've come into the kitchen, for it's been
my room, just as the parlor has been hers,
although it's larger here, and the high ceiling
takes what the firelight throws and muddies it
with shadows, or the shadowings of light,
a fluttering I always think is like
what water throws, reflected off canals.

And now, the papers. Bundled. Tied with ribbon.
And what's this? Fur? No, finer. Hair. But not
what I'd expect, a lock of brownish curls.
No, more a mess, a pitiful remembrance.
The fire is small, but surely it will do.
And he can help it grow, a bit of kindling
from hair as legendary as her eyes,
but not as frightening. Let me unfold
the first of these. Thin. Carefully creased. Aqua.

My dear Miss Juliana Bordereau—

Let us be sisters—though I am a man—
more intimate than lovers and more pure,
sharing our secrets here, more guessed at than
believed or known. Let gossip be our cure
when we fall ill with wistfulness of love.
For love shall pluck our tunes, and swell our breeze
when the sweet evening seasons with its clove
and whispers are the ripples of great seas.

We'll both wear pantaloons, doff parasols,
and stroll upon the Riva. Are you shocked
that we may waltz our way through the masked balls
with nothing from our open faces blocked?

Humor me, now, with sisterly affection,
pleased how long-standing is this fresh connection.

—Your most attentive servant, Jeffrey Aspern

Once I was fond of taking a promenade
at my aunt's bidding, and my velvet hat

tried to fly off, but gracious, it was bound
by a red ribbon underneath my chin!
Why would he want a sister? Had he none?
You wouldn't talk so foolishly to me
if you could answer, looking up from reading.
I'd love to watch you reading silently
in this dark room. The paper isn't silent—
it catches at the edges, and I hold on
as long as I can, watch it burn, and drop it.

    My dear Miss Juliana—

       The Virgin Mary's so desirable
in Venice, baring her breast with a slight
smile and a full-eyed stare. I'd take the call
myself and worship at her shrine of light.

       But yours will do, my saint of the canal.
No, not a saint, but living, like a sprig
with a sun's bloom, a burst below the wall
of a closed garden, wild, but not too big.

       Is it your cloister I have floated by
in the black shell that creaks beside the walkway?
The blossoms, when I suck in, make me sigh.
What would we both, permitted, in our talk say?

       Pardon my manners. They are New World, crude
as proper savages who must go nude.

                —Yours, J.A.

Heavens, I shouldn't want the Virgin naked!
But I have seen the pictures. Holy enough,

though I must wonder how the model stood it.
Certainly he was far more than direct.
Perhaps he teased her. But she never said.
And the green shade she wore to spare her eyes
was, I suppose, her mourning garb for him.
(You know it well now—dream of it, I'm sure.)
Yes, I am right to follow her instructions
and do what she would want. This correspondence
is hardly public. Too strange for strange eyes,
even yours, the strangest I have known.

Dear Juliana—

Custom is nothing but a bill of duties,
taxing to anyone who tries to smuggle
silk negligées from well-known harbor cities
or jewelry that would make a countess wiggle.

"It simply isn't done here." What a motto
to force on those whose freedom isn't sparing,
who love in stanzas, lavish rooms where sotto
voce *comes not from cautiousness but daring!*

Husbands are dull, like planters who have hired
farmhands to cultivate the land they own
but don't possess. Their wives are worse off, squired
by elderly associates through the town.

If secrets chose, what lady wouldn't take
her garden worked in nightly by a rake?

—Yours sincerely, Jeffrey

If you were sitting here, now, I'd be silent,
watching the firelight on your eyes, as you
took in the words Aunt Juliana wanted
burned in the hearth. A heart that would not burn?
I can't remember when she said it. Often.
Oh, you would know. It's something you could edit,
like my life here. And we could burn them once
you'd copied them, or learned them all by heart,
and let me honor what I promised her—
or would the inky scratches matter more?
You were so generous, with all your money,
but she believed that it was merely greed
that could spend lavishly on drafty rooms.
I did speak up for you. And she approved,
as long as she would not be present then.
For she could not abide you, from the start,
except for my sake, and my future's sake.

My Juliana—

*A husband marries that he might forget
the woman with his name—no problems of
"Now who the devil was the girl I met
in Dorsoduro?" (Learning by heart is love.)
He grumbles at domesticating claims
and goes off drinking in the nearest tavern,
where made-up women offer made-up names
and pleasure is the party picked to govern.*

*Learning by heart is love, and memory
is what I offer, not a ritual
of chores—obligatory, no days free—
fixed in a sampler on a parlor wall.*

Remembering is all I ask of you
and all I promise. Do I vow? I do.

—Ever yours now, Jeffrey

You know I can't think ill of you. I can't!
I like considering these papers ours,
our papers. We're in league together. Were.
Somehow the mirror's darker than the room
when I look up, away from all the glowing,
and doesn't catch the ripples from the fire.

My Juliana—

Getting lost is a solace of the blest,
a sweet prerogative, through turning lanes
and sudden bridges as I take the crest
and look out at dark water, darkened panes.

It matters little what had been my plans.
Though spoiled, they have been spared, and I can go
where I had not expected, over spans
that link the known world to what I don't know.

And so I chanced to meet you, with no thought
but bad transactions in my jostled head,
ripe for surprise, a burglar who is caught
napping within a house, in his own bed.

And so you met me on a mapless route
from nowhere, which I knew, and found me out.

—Always your own, Jeffrey

How slow it catches. But days go more slowly,
light and dark and light and hardly moving—
I rock in my embroidered chair, front, back,
the needlepoint my own, but the chair hers.
I like it better in this large, clean room.

 Juliana—

   Many a pair at a masked ball
   slip off their masks at Carnival
   and dance upon the Grand Canal.

       —May my boat call?

               —Jeffrey

I'd rather dance, were I asked, in a great hall
lit by the torches lifted up by Moors,
painted or living, tall or stumpy as dwarfs.
I can remember flames upon the marble
glowing against the shine of many colors.
A light like this one, in the marble hearth
where usually a kettle hangs or meat
roasts on a spit, or used to, years ago.

 My Juliana—

   I wish you thought it practical to swim
   instead of strolling. Granted, we would make
   our way more slowly, aching in each limb,
   than boats that would glide by and leave their wake.

   We'd navigate like otters through the marsh
   when the sun died, sputtering like a gas jet—

except we wouldn't have to dive for fish
and get ourselves entangled in a net.

We'd stroke and kick as others took a stroll
along the fondamenta, *tipped their hats*
or waved their fans to greet us. And we'd haul
ourselves up water steps, wet as drenched cats—
but happy, drying soon enough to use
two seats in Florian's and read the news.

—Lovingly, your Jeffrey

I think I fluttered when you said "Miss Tina"
and I flushed then, I'm sure, for I could feel
the heat upon my cheeks. I couldn't think
a word. I couldn't find the proper one.
I couldn't recollect what others said
to a kind boarder's face. What did I say?
The words go by me, as they always have.

Sweet Juliana—

I like to think of legends happening here
in this wet place, where bodies must crowd near—
as Tristan, rising to his messages,
parts the gauze curtain, unsashes, and says,
"My love, it is an agony of heaven
that here, by marble banks, we two are given
loving and leaving, dalliance and dying,
to learn to make love as we first learn lying."
Their innocence was part of their deceit—
as was their childish craving for the sweet.

And now I'm hungry too, for delicacies
that smell like your perfumes in the salt breeze,
and want to stuff myself— No, don't be coarse
and brush fine cheekbones raw and red, or worse.
The sweetest breeze is indoors, when you breathe,
your fingers through my hair my laurel wreath.

—Meet me again soon, Jeffrey

I too would be yours—and my belongings,
old longings, my long lease in this old place . . .
I came here to be educated soundly,
and so with evenings, taking the Piazza,
the fans inside a hostess's salon,
and the smart talk, all the parties, dull plays
in brilliant theaters, full of the finest chatter.
How many hands took mine? Yes, just as many
released the gentle grip, it felt so feeble.
I turned away before I meant to turn—
as you, perhaps, did when you turned and left.
Aunt Juliana sneered. When Mr. Aspern
clasped her thin waist, she didn't flinch. And when
his lips met hers, I don't believe she shrank.

Juliana, loveliest—

Your lips, like bees upon the flowers, lit
on my own, delicate, though they could sting
when all the fragments of the lamplights flit
on the canal, breaking and gathering.

But you have emptied me. Sweetness is gone
from hours of staying up in solitude.

And I'm immobile, rooted, fixed upon
a balcony that passing boats have viewed.

But, really, life's not bad at this hotel,
although the bed is like a doge's barge.
I'd love to say I'm ailing, but I'm well
and never sleep on mattresses that large.

So, if I'm still your orchid, please be quick
to come again for gathering, and pick.

—Jeffrey, lowliest

Aunt Juliana's teaching me comprised
what to withhold in human intercourse:
the kinds of flowers, dress materials,
manners at table and the way to step
into a rocking boat, lifting my hem,
the authors it was proper to admire.
Her conduct—how could scandal threaten her?
She never did a bad thing in her life.

My Juliana, dearest one—

I prize the piercing of your eyes
            as martyrs love the lance
        pricking them clear to heaven.
            Your glance
        has hit direct and driven
my body so intensely that it dies.

But oddly, I remain, and you
            look just as piercingly,
        fixing me in your vision.

You see
with no hint of derision,
a look that feels as soft as cushions do.

—J.A., Ca' Giustinian

I know that look. Her eyes are terrible!
Were. Nothing penetrates, no, nothing burns
the way her disapproval felt. Not even
this fire I keep on feeding in the hearth,
half on the grate, half off. I poke it some.
You know that look. Your own was horrified
when she fell back, half dying, in my arms.
Your look, before you parted, was the same.
Discovery disgusts you? Yes, I see,
and now it's low. I'm running out of scraps.

My patient Juliana—

You might imagine that I love to pose
and have my picture taken by a hand
with watercolors, proud of my fine nose
and steady as a schooner on dry land.

But my legs twitch, I feel an urge to go,
and meditation's better done alone,
in a cool room, than in a studio.
My fingers want to drum. I am not stone.

So, I confess, I'm restless to the core,
and, as you well know, only a miniature
is finished soon enough. Oils would mean more
hours to execute—and to endure.

But as the artist was your father, I
am glad I stilled my flesh—and let paints dry.

—Restless, Jeffrey

Relations! What was hers is now all mine,
and my possessions—I would be possessed
and you could have these documents. What's left.
We'd leave this drafty house, the smelly water
I let my hand drift down in—years ago,
or was it when your boatmen rowed us both
to the Piazza?—leave the damp and dank
and winds that gather up and make us cross
and ride a steamer to— The fire is lovely.
Nothing will keep you here, but I shall stay.

My Juliana—

Now you're alarmed. And have you heard of others?
A countess here, a washerwoman there,
no matter if they're debutantes or mothers
with tattered rags or pearls in their coiffed hair?

Explaining pains the guiltless too. It bothers
my one love, you, and so let me declare
my soul is not my own. You must be liable
for what it does. It's yours. That's undeniable.

—Faithfully, your Jeffrey

Something happened between the two of them—
or everything, which I could not imagine
beyond these words, too saucy, too outré,

yet oddly like the prettiest of children.
When nothing happens, that too is a plot.
I always like the ingénue in plays
who stays as innocent and never changes,
except for how she's costumed, scene by scene.
I envy all the nuns in their black frocks
who walk, not stroll, along the lanes and bridges.
Where is my country? What is my religion?
You who could tell me tripped away with mutters,
and what you said in those late messages,
posted from the Veneto, seemed the same
as notices from an official bureau.
Nothing. Yet, certainly, I must prepare
to meet you when you call again, if only
to ask the porter to divest your rooms,
but at your pleasure, as the maid shall serve you.

Dearest Juliana—

> *I glimpse the future, and it isn't ours—*
> *an arrow's arc that's plotted on a graph*
> *but ends at its apex, shot from a tower's*
> *archers at sport, piercing a bird in half.*
> *Is that so bad? I'd play through our last hours*
> *and fall in a canal, to make you laugh.*

> *Time is what we've had, and now it seizes us*
> *and wrenches us, in exile, from what pleases us.*

> *—Ever, Jeffrey*

If I have seemed coquettish, please forgive me
for feeling I, perhaps, was being wooed:

you sought me out so eagerly, and lived
more dearly than this old house might deserve.

> *You love me—yes?—for what I am, and not*
> *what critics say I should be. Well, the fact*
> *is that I'm restless, fearful to be caught*
> *like a snared parrot. Dearest, I have packed*
> *my books and wardrobe. Leaving, love, means what?*
> *My picture, like a traitorous doge's, blacked?*

> *(How serious, I wonder, would life's drama be*
> *if we could not mix pathos into comedy?)*

I miss the flowers you sent up to us,
though I would never press them, nor preserve them,
collecting what is only good when fresh—
unlike Aunt Juliana and her verses.
Well, perhaps they keep a little better,
I couldn't say. She didn't tell me either,
evenings when we sat and read. Could you?
She seldom spoke, in truth, of Mr. Aspern
but settled by the secretary, hushed,
or by the fireplace, leafing carefully.
I shall not read the lot to you, but some.

> *The dying sun has torched a path on water*
> *in the great basin named after St. Mark.*
> *And I must die away from you, no matter*
> *that the flames glow until it's nearly dark.*
> *Fire burns itself as well. The painter's daughter*
> *now must picture every fluttering spark*
> *and how it rises. Think of that, love, cherishing*
> *the heat and light we kindled, not their perishing.*

Exits, to me, are new as entrances—
and just as temporary. Settling down
is but returning to my regular life,
different, yes, but not so different,
like one whose favorite chair has been restuffed.
I never need a word to know her words.
And she was kindest, even to you, in silence—
but you could not endure it. Like my talk.

        J.—

        I have to leave because I love too near—
        at all's a bafflement—but, love, it's you
        who shoo me to my wanderings from here
        to who knows where—home?—continents won't do
        in satisfying what I've known but forfeit,
        wishing I were constant—yet I must leave—
        a wedding coat, on me, would have a poor fit—
        better a black arm-band on my coat sleeve.

        If anybody seeks what I send you,
        let them be thwarted—as we've been fulfilled,
        immersed in one another, wet clear through—
        be my executor. Spend what I've willed.

        If anybody wants these scribbles, turn them
        over to my favorite critic. Burn them.

                                    —J.

Why does it matter so? Why do you seem
so eager to pursue the gentleman
as if he were a lady? Or you were.

It must be more than papers you pursued!
You wouldn't tell me, would you? No, you couldn't,
even though a word, a smile, a nod
would have resounded in my ears, and you
could have had your way, yes, but you turned then
and fled as if I'd dallied with your virtue.
I'll never understand, and yet I know.

Juliana—

> *If what we have, our brave love, now must finish,*
> *let it go. Try to. It will not diminish.*

—Jeffrey

My, what a heap of ash, the logs and sheets
mingling but different, now that they are powder.
My cheeks feel dry, but soft enough, at least
to my own touch. Your boat may come tomorrow
or not, it doesn't matter, I must wait.
I shall stand—not here—out in the hallway,
and bid goodbye and wish you well and smile,
or try to, offering my hand to shake
(at least, for this time, one that won't be spurned),
and offer the assistance of my staff,
turning away, for this is now my future,
the legacy that Juliana's willed me—
not money that you paid in rent, your gold,
your hovering to meet me in the hall,
but this last look. I shall not say "Farewell."

IV

First Trip to Venice

My first night in the city, I went out
    and scouted through the colonnades
for courtesans in mini-skirts who'd meet
    my timid looks with smiles and nods.

I thought they would be floating, a slow fleet
    of cleavages and hair, perfumes
that mingled with sea breezes and smelled sweet
    as naked bodies in pink rooms.

I'd seen the paintings with expectant looks
    on their warm faces and felt sure
I'd find them if I wandered through dark nooks
    of the Piazza, out of the glare—

but I returned to the Atlantico
    and my huge room always alone,
knowing I could have sneaked a woman through
    the stuffy lobby, her hand in mine.

Nothing came true from my imagining.
    I always had to be surprised
by the real, sudden flow of everything.
    Nothing occurred as fantasized.

I also had the notion that I'd go
    to the Rialto Bridge and write
a poem that would change my life. I'd know
    what to say in the noon sunlight.

It never happened, though I climbed the bridge
    and gazed down each side. But the rush
of light on broken waves and the stone edge
    muted me. And so did the push

of passersby and shoppers, the Venetians
    pausing to chat. I loved the wives,
baskets in hands, who looked like restored Titians,
    tinted with shadows from stone eaves.

I loved the rippling light the canal tossed
    over the surfaces of stone.
It skittered on the faces as they passed
    up the broad steps and then down.

It wasn't, after all, what I expected.
    But light, water, and a brusque wind
won me instead of winning them, connected
    to everything I had not planned.

THE CEMETERY ISLAND

1. At Ezra Pound's Grave, 1994

Still rocking from the vaporetto ride
I wander,
                camera for amulet, past
blocks of stacked tombs:
                photographs behind glass
                and sconces of bouquets.

Lost in long alleys, I turn
                and stumble upon
cypresses in the walled plot
                for foreigners
        (who isn't in this true Serenissima?)
                overgrown with heaps
of broken statues, bashed slabs, crosses
                                in pieces.

At last
        (since my first trip to Venice in 1972)
                                I arrive:
                an ivy raft
with a tree for mast, a hatch of carved marble.

I snap a laurel leaf from the green crown
and press it in a currency receipt,
        wipe dirt from the name
        (and what admirer does otherwise?)
                the slab
flattened to the earth's curve,
                        trap door
                sealed to the underworld.

2. What Thou Lovest Well, 1997

Now that Olga Rudge has moved in, the plot's arranged in
a family portrait: two tilted slabs, like name plates on an
office desk, framed in a white border with a half-moon
extension in front, geometrically Palladian. A carved urn
with a dead plant sits in the semi-circle. Sawed-off stumps
poke out near the rear line segment, the earth cracked from
all the beautiful days in the treacherous lagoon.

3. At Joseph Brodsky's Grave, 1997

There's a white cross, with pebbles on the arms
and peak, more offerings heaped up below—
a vase of daisies, a blue can with terms
in Hebrew lettering, a candle's glow
inside (and in a red translucent jar
with a gold lid)—for this last seminar.

How did he manage to be buried here,
the lucky stiff? Unsanctioned by the chaplain,
apart from where the other Russians are,
Jewish by birth and Ezra's fan, light rippling
through cypresses, the push of the lagoon
against pocked Istrian marble, a surge of brine.

So now the island has a grove of bards,
a college of silence, where the shade refreshes
and lizards skitter under hidden birds.
A vaporetto's diesel motor hushes
when it approaches past the crumbling walls,
and sparrows comment with their quietest calls.

LI PO IN CHINATOWN

Why do I live among gray tenements?
Florist shops are in flower
and water flows from the hydrants.
Why do the storefronts beam, the radios hum?

My friends have pushed off
down Canal Street, past vegetable hawkers
with string-tied bunches of leeks
and bok choy, past quail eggs in paper cartons.

In bright light, a man with a fresh apron
brushes a chopping block clean.
Displayed in his butcher shop window,
pullets droop like wineskins.

I mutter between the pagodas
of telephone booths, reeling from the wine
we poured in teacups
red with hummingbirds.

Now, the wind gone, banners above Mott Street
drop and sag. I'd like to dangle
in a hammock like that, sleeping off
our parting, the ring of *so long*.

BAMBOO

for Ruth McClure

1.

The committee at Lingnan
sent you a scroll, a landscape
in memory of your husband:

student of bamboo, carver
of bamboo instruments, who used to trace
characters in his palm before he slept.

Mountains half in mist, waterfalls
flowing from the sky,
calligraphy as thin as feelers:

it had the look
of T'ang brushwork, except for
the delicately traced powerlines.

2.

Crane legs, heads
tucked under feathers—the grove
of bamboo ruffling in the wind:

all of his might went into clutching
the closed bottle of pills.
Then the sky filled with wings.

The pipes dripped noisily after so much rain.
When you called "What is it?"
no one answered.

3.

Listen hard, as you always do.
Crickets are beginning
their monotonous, endless rounds.

Look through the twilight
to the near dark of the grove:
even from the porch you hear the rush and rattle.

It settles you, dwelling among culms
and crescent-shaped leaves he planted
in Maryland, the farthest north

bamboo had ever flourished. When he died,
the smell of the cedar still flowed, and the reeds
still bent with rain. You listened and still

looked deep into the grove
he lost himself within, the shoots
of tree-grass, "symbol of devotion."

Now the lines so light
and deft on the scroll could be
his own strokes, or the long streaks of bamboo.

Pausing to look at it,
even years from now in a distant state,
you'll feel a breeze, and twilight drifting in.

BEARD

My mother wants to see me again. That means she'd like me
    to shave off my beard.
She points her thumb at the dark portrait of a bearded man,
    whose name is Caleb,
and calls him "Spinach Face." Gazing over the fluted sofa
    and butler's table,
he's a mystery, though we've visited his grave: an obelisk
    with wreaths at the base.
A shield on his marker bears the inscription "A Man Strong
    for the Right."
But what, I wonder, could that mean in a county where slavery
    was legal for most of his lifetime?
What did he do for a living? I learn from property records and
    census reports
that Caleb Shepherd owned windmills, a half-share in a
    schooner, and worked as a miller.
Now I can see him: standing by sacks of meal that someone
    he employed, most likely black,
heaved onto a wagon that clattered through unpaved streets
    toward docks on the river
where stevedores, also black, stacked them on barges for
    transport up the Chesapeake.
I don't know what this bearded ancestor might have construed
    as "right,"
with the blades of his windmill spinning from gusts off the
    bay,
and wooden gears turning to pulverize grain, and cereal dust
    rising in the mill
and settling on his wool trousers and in his graying beard
    hairs.

On the packet boat to Baltimore, passengers mistook him for
    Robert E. Lee,
with his beard and aquiline nose, though the General had died
    years before.
I hope he didn't respond by smiling and touching the brim of
    his planter's hat
but had the decency to blush for the misidentification, at least
    in part
to deny the cause he never fought for, to assert, "No, ma'am,
    I'm only a miller."
My mother isn't impressed. "Just once, please, just once
    before I die."

SUICIDE BRIDGE

We're deep in the county now,
elbows on oilcloth, Cabin Creek
fiery with late light
like a wrench testing a Die Hard's charge.
We're the restaurant's lone patrons,
so far, and we're gloating
about the crab bisque we ordered.
It turns out the waitress
is a distant cousin. The bridge nearby
arches on trestles, white
guardrails over a slim neck
of brackish water. Boys are piloting
a johnboat, smoking cigarettes
as their cranky Evinrude sputters.
It turns out that, sure enough,
a few people have perished
leaping from the bridge—though one of them
shot himself first before falling.
My mother enjoys the name, never mind
that her father, at the onset of the New Deal,
poisoned himself. She says,
"They pumped his stomach, but he couldn't
stop hemorrhaging," as if the surgeons
had somehow done him in. She remembers him
huddled in the rock garden, weeping,
choking down a bottle's worth of sleeping pills.
But surely that's wrong for 1933.
I puzzle it out in flashes.
Days before, he had tried to hurtle
from the attic window, catching
his trousers on the sill,

but they pulled him back, the fool,
high enough only
to fracture some bones, to knock the wind out.
And who can say why?
A fire in his dry goods store,
a last will bequeathed to hearth fire:
who knows what spark ignites, what fizzles,
what catches light
then flickers out to blackness?
Steaming with the glory of blue crabs,
our bisque appears, thick
in a milky broth. We notice
a fire across the water, now blackened,
close to a pier and what looks like a gazebo.
Should it be burning, we ask.

How It Matters

for Eric Pankey

A robin that never sang *cheer up, cheerily*
built a nest in the scraggly juniper
beside our front stoop, the maples still bare
as she set to work, flying in tufts
and wet clumps and red kite string.
She roosted there, in a bush
as patchy as an old zoo animal—
with so few berries I could count them all—
through wind gusts that shook her
and downpours that drenched her dun coat.
She looked miserable, slick and matted,
but never budged.
                    A single bird was hatched.
A few weeks later, I saw a fledgling
crushed on the sidewalk. It may have been
the same bird, I don't know. I think
of the mother's endurance
and indifference, patient in her makeshift nest
with a gap underneath.
                    I think of the boredom
of doughboys, posted in muddy trenches,
not firing, but waiting for a culmination,
drops of rainwater trickling off their helmets.
I don't know—maybe it matters
that we suffer, without explanation.
Maybe effacement is our truest self image.
I don't know is my motto, my refrain,
which I mutter to no one in particular, denying
what I believe.
                    Yet I see the tired soldiers
cupping cigarettes in the damp air

to light them, to hide the glow signalling
their position.
                    I don't know how weather
holds us in its easy grip, how the elements
trick us into faith, how the seasons take us in.
I don't know how it matters, how it all
makes sense.
                  "I don't know," I muttered
in a stuffy train compartment
six people were supposed to sleep in.
A long day in Italy. I grumbled to myself
about misfortune, about my failure to find a room,
missing the sights while looking for accommodations.
It was wet and hot. But at the window,
a boy with enormous eyeglasses
stood as we pulled from the terminal,
gazing at the platform,
the grime, the factories, the crooked skyline,
and whispered, almost like a song
I didn't know, "Ciao, bella Milano."

John Drury teaches English and creative writing at the University of Cincinnati. His previous books include *The Disappearing Town,* also published by Miami University Press, *The Poetry Dictionary,* and *Creating Poetry.* The title poem of this new collection received the Bernard F. Conners Prize from *The Paris Review.* Other poems have appeared in *The American Poetry Review, The Beloit Poetry Journal, The New Republic, Poetry Northwest, Shenandoah, The Southern Review, Western Humanities Review,* and other periodicals, as well as in an anthology, *Ravishing DisUnities: Real Ghazals in English.* Educated at the State University of New York at Stony Brook, Johns Hopkins University, and the University of Iowa, he now lives in Cincinnati with his wife, Laurie Henry, and their children, Eric and Rebecca.